Red Flags: The Dating Red Flag Checklist to Spot a Narcissist, Abuser or Manipulator Before They Hurt You

Lauren Kozlowski

Published by Escape The Narcissist, 2019.

While every precaution has been taken in the preparation of this book, the publisher assumes no responsibility for errors or omissions, or for damages resulting from the use of the information contained herein.

RED FLAGS: THE DATING RED FLAG CHECKLIST TO SPOT A NARCISSIST, ABUSER OR MANIPULATOR BEFORE THEY HURT YOU

First edition. May 14, 2019.

Copyright © 2019 Lauren Kozlowski.

ISBN: 978-1393271536

Written by Lauren Kozlowski.

Table of Contents

Dating Red Flags: The Dating Red Flag Checklist to Spot a Narcissist, Abuser or Manipulator Before They Hurt You

By Lauren Kozlowski

Before you go ahead and read this book, I'd like to answer a few questions you may have, just to make sure this book is for you:

What are dating red flags?

Red flags are indicators that something in your relationship needs to be questioned or otherwise validated. These often serve as clues that the relationship may be trouble in the future. Red flags are behaviors, actions or words that shouldn't be overlooked should you bear witness to them - they're there to warn you of the possible toxicity this relationship may bring.

I'm not dating, I'm in a relationship. Is this book going to help me?

This book is aimed towards those who are in the beginning phases of their relationship, or the 'dating' stage, to be used as a cautionary guide to snuff out any toxicity before it goes too far. However, if you're in a long-term relationship, and you're looking for validation that you're witnessing red flags or you're living with an abuser, this book can be of help to you.

Are you a therapist/psychologist/coach? What are your credentials for writing this book?

No, I'm not. I'm a former victim of a malignant narcissist, and I was brought up by a violent, narcissistic father who I now believe to be malignant. He would relentlessly abuse, belittle and berate my mother as I was growing up, and when I began dating, I stepped right into the snare of a toxic, cruel narcissist. I remained in this abusive relationship for seven years, and once I escape his clutches, I exposed myself to the dating world once again. This book will be based on my own toxic relationships, the relationships of others who've been through the hell of an abusive relationship and the newfound intuition and integrity we've walked away with because of what we've experienced.

****

Hopefully, I've answered any questions you may have, and if you're certain that this book is for you, welcome inside!

****

Dating can be an emotional minefield, especially in today's world of ghosting, gaslighting and confusing online relationships. It seems that finding a mate isn't as breezy as those Hollywood romantic comedies make out; we need to be careful of users, liars, cheats, and manipulators. We have to dodge the catfish and weave past the compulsive liars, making sure we avoid the obsessive cyberstalkers who won't take **no** for an answer.

In short, you have to have your wits about you when you're dating.

I may sound cynical and pessimistic, and you might assume that I'm full of distrust and that I'm incredibly hardened towards other people.

However, whilst I may have traits of pessimism in me, I do trust until proven otherwise and I'm open to getting to know all kinds of new and wonderful people. Instead of calling myself cynical, I'd prefer to say I have a lot of integrity - and I expect the same back from a potential partner.

I'm like this because, for a long period of my life, *I wasn't* - I was low on self-esteem, I was beaten down, trodden on and afraid of making life choices. I was in a relationship with a narcissist who also had a tendency to be violent towards me. I believe he was a malignant narcissist, torturing me with his cruel words and often just-as-cruel fists. I was manipulated, constantly lied to and regularly cheated on.

I was gaslighted to the point I would believe it if my abusive ex told me the sky was orange - even though I could see with my own eyes that it was blue.

I would be fearful of saying or doing the wrong thing in case I upset my abuser, which would cause him to unleash his incredibly hurtful and wicked side.

Of course, it wasn't like this in the beginning. I didn't fall for an abusive monster. I fell for a kind, charming, funny and charismatic man; one who knew what to say and do to make me feel butterflies in my stomach and weak at the knees. He love-bombed me until I was his entirely.

However, if I'd stopped for a moment, I'd notice the huge red flags that were waving in front of me. Perhaps, at the time, I did notice some of them but chose to believe that I was being silly or it was just me being paranoid - something we've likely all been guilty of when starting out a new relationship that we *really* want to work out. We choose to believe the manipulative words of our soon-to-be abuser over our own primal gut instinct.

Red flags serve as a warning to us in the early stages of a would-be abusive relationship. Whilst an abuser can mask their cruel side whilst in the beginning stages of a relationship, they do give away some telltale signs of their future intentions. I want to help you avoid falling into a manipulative, abusive or narcissistic relationship by guiding you to understanding what these red flags are, leaving you knowing when to preserve yourself from a volatile relationship.

Some red flags are hard to work out. It may seem like your new partner has the best intentions for you by being 'overprotective' when, really, they're setting the stage for their possessive and controlling ways. You may think that your date is looking out for you by warning you about your 'untrustworthy' friends when in reality, they're readying you for a life of isolation.

I wrote this short guide as something of a handbook for its readers. If you've been in an abusive relationship or if you've been mistreated and manipulated, I hope this book will serve you well when you vet your potential future partners. If you've not experienced the horrors of an abusive partner, this book will also serve you, too, although I do mention my experiences with abuse throughout this book, as well as the stories of some of the women I got to know via a support group. This may make this short read a little more heavy hitting than you'd like.

As a former victim of abuse, I know that just being in an abusive relationship doesn't make you invincible to the users, liars, and cheats. When I got back on the dating scene after seven years with an abuser, I was fragile. I had my walls up for sure, but I was still susceptible to the manipulation and deceit that had plagued me for years. I was still under the belief that I was nothing; *a burden, an emotional wreck, unhinged, damaged goods...* So, it's safe to say I did get burned yet again when I put myself back out there.

Only, instead of accepting the vile, cruel and nefarious treatment from my potential suitors, I began to take heed of the red flags that would present themselves. I began to understand what these red flags represented, how they would creep up covertly and what those flags meant for my future with that specific person. I started to trust my gut, and the word 'paranoid' would no longer be part of my self-talk vocabulary.

I'd like this book to be your go-to when you feel like your gut is telling you something different to your love interest, or when you feel like something is amiss with your new partner but need some guidance on what. The checklist in this book has been compiled through my own experiences, the experiences of those who have been through abusive relationships and also from the input of various survivors of abuse who were kind enough to tell me their stories.

Red Flag #1 - Withholding Affection From You

When you first get into a new relationship or begin dating someone new, the first phase is usually always filled with affection, attention, and compliments. This can make it incredibly hard to see who's the real deal and who wants to snare you in and take advantage of you. At the beginning of a relationship, your partner is always the 'perfect' guy or girl; they hook you in with their abundance of adoration.

However, this is how abusive and, particularly narcissistic, relationships can begin. *But how can I tell if their affection is genuine or just a set-up for heartache,* you're asking?

People with a healthy outlook on their relationship can be relied upon to be consistent with their feelings and emotions. Of course, we're all human and can get a little tetchy and upset now and again, but for the most part, emotionally healthy people will be reliable in their affection and attention towards you.

Something that should serve as a red flag is if they begin to withhold or retract that attention. If you find your partner has become uninterested and somewhat reclusive towards you, pay attention to this. Our natural reaction is to chase the love and adoration they once bestowed upon us, making us appear desperate, needy and clingy.

This is the reaction a narcissist would want to achieve from withholding the affection they once gave to you so freely. If this is something you've experienced, notice this as a red flag and proceed with caution: are you the one always initiating contact? Are you the one who chases intimacy and affection? Is it you who always arranges dates or time together? If so, it may be that you're fuelling your partner's narcissistic tendencies.

By taking away the affection and love you had gotten so used to, your partner may be enjoying the boosts of confidence and ego your chasing is giving them. For a narcissist, this would top up their narcissistic fuel tank, because all the chasing and fawning over them would, in their toxic mind, be undermining you and your self-esteem. This, in turn, boosts their own.

Red Flag #2 - Over-Communication

It's endearing and sweet when our new partner is constantly texting us, posting on our social media and calling us to see what we're up to. We might even be guilty of this ourselves - texting from the moment we wake up to the time we go to sleep isn't uncommon when we're in the throes of a new and exciting relationship.

So, where do we draw the line?

This one needs to be gauged by you and your own instinct. If your gut tells you the person your dating is too much - too many social media posts to your wall, too many missed calls one after the other, repeated texts even though they know you're busy - then you need to listen to your gut.

I met my friend Katie, a former victim of a verbally abusive and controlling relationship, through a social media page dedicated to victims of emotional abuse. We bonded over our love of art and our eerily similar abusive relationships. As we shared our stories with one another, she recalled to me how this red flag should have been the warning sign she needed to call it quits before she dived head-first into the relationship. She was kind enough to let me use her story as Red Flag #3:

When I met my ex, he was the most caring, sweet man you could imagine. He'd shower me with compliments, songs and little poems that he'd written just for me. Whilst, at times, I felt a little uncomfortable receiving them (he'd watch me open and read his poems in front of him, waiting for my reaction), I thought that his intentions were pure.

However, things began to go from keen-but-sweet to (what I now view as) a big red flag. The 'good morning' text became two, which became three, which became four - if I didn't reply straight away, it would become missed phone calls or texts demanding where I am and what I'm doing. He would justify these by saying he was 'worried' something had happened to me.

The daily posts to my social media telling me how special I was had become embarrassingly riddled with compliments and over-sharing of our intimate times. What I brushed off as him being proud to be with me and wanting to show it off was, in reality, him claiming me as his own and warning others off.

The songs and poems he presented me with became more elaborate and full of commitment and future planning. Once, when I was away for work, he posted me letters every day, which he assumed would be ready and waiting for me when I arrived home. My mother was taking care of my flat whilst I was away for the week, so she picked them up for me, and due to the look of the letters assumed they were junk and shoved them in my 'junk' pile ready for me to sort when I was home. I didn't pay too much attention to the 'junk' pile and just threw it in the bin when it overflowed. As such, I binned all but one of his letters, unknowingly.

This filled him with rage. He was incensed that I hadn't gotten his love letters and even accused me of having another man round at my flat who must have 'intercepted' them. When he eventually die (after many weeks) believe me that I'd mistakenly binned them, his reply should also have waved that huge red flag in my face. He said, 'don't worry, I photocopied all of the letters anyway. I can still give you them.'

True to his word, he had photocopied them all. He'd dated them all. The shortest was four (double-sided) pages long. I read them in front of him, almost skimming across the words but trying to react in a way that appeased him - I tried to appear happy and grateful when really I felt uneasy.

Over-communication and over flattery should be a red flag for a controlling and manipulative relationship. It suggests the other person has a need to reel you in tightly, which isn't a good start - you should be free to flourish at the beginning of a relationship not forced to abide by their strict communication regime. I spent four years with a controlling bully because I didn't listen to my gut or have the will to see the red flags in front of me.

Red Flag #3 - Deep Feelings Early On

The person who I'm now engaged to initially told me that they loved me after nine weeks. To some, that may be early, to others it may be the right time and some people may recoil at how soon it was. For me, I also felt it was too soon. It did startle me little, and it did give me a slight red flag jitter. However, it was my reaction to this that helped me decide if this was a genuine red flag to be wary of.

I told him it was too soon for me. I told him that, although I cared about him, I couldn't say it back - not *ever*, just not right now. I mentioned that I felt it was a little too soon, and I told him I was hesitant to move so deeply so quickly.

Although this did wound him slightly, I knew I had to be honest. Not only for me but for him, too. I set my expectations, I told him I'd been hurt before and I'd already said that I'd like to take things slow. I could absolutely see myself falling for him, and I *was* falling for him, but 'too much too soon' is a red flag I'd already been all too familiar with.

His reaction and actions over the subsequent months showed me that his declaration of love was genuine. He accepted my reaction and didn't force me into anything, and he didn't make me feel guilty or like I was 'bad' for not feeling the same as him. He didn't profess his love over and over, thus making me uncomfortable or like I had to say it back. He allowed things to go at my pace, which is what a healthy relationship offers: compromise meaning not always getting what you want right away, as well as a deep consideration of your partner's feelings.

When I was ready, I reciprocated those feelings and the rest is history.

However, declaration of deep feelings early on is very often a red flag. I was cautious when my fiancee mentioned love after nine weeks. I treated it as a red flag, and my advice to others is to treat it like one, too. Whilst it worked out for me this time, every other early declaration of love toward me had ended in heartbreak. They were controllers, manipulators and serial cheats - I had every right to be cautious of someone else professing their deep feelings for me so early on.

My advice is to air on the side of caution if someone is calling you 'the one' or their 'soulmate' after a few dates. If your other half is swooning with words like this so soon, it can be an indicator of someone who does this frequently for their own gains. Tread carefully, and be aware of the reasons manipulators use this 'lovebombing' technique; to exert their control and power over their victim once they have them sucked in.

Reg Flag #4 - They Lie and Use Excuses Freely

It may take you a little while to pick up on this - after all, we can't always know when someone is lying to us, but our intuition and our gut will always figure this out for us in the end.

Be cautious of any potential suitor who lies or has an excuse for everything. Be extra cautious of someone who makes up lies and excuses when there isn't any real or apparent reason to do so. For example, they're not lying to spare your feelings or making up excuses for something that doesn't require them to do so - they're offering up their untruths out of habit. This is something that should have the red flags waving frantically at you if you're experiencing it.

It can be your initial reaction to confront a liar or serial excuser about their behavior, but keep in mind that they're adept at this game - they can most probably make up lies and excuses quicker than you can process them and question them. It's often also a smaller part of their bigger manipulation plan; to have you second guessing yourself and doubting your own recollection of events or conversations.

Another common bad habit of the liars and excusers is to blame other people for their misgivings. If your other half can't admit when they've done wrong and the blame is always shifted to another person (maybe even you), then this is something you can't brush under the carpet and simply accept. If your other half can never be at fault, regardless of the evidence stacked against them that suggests otherwise, then allow this to trigger the mental red flags. Consider how much time your partner spends explaining, rationalizing and blaming their actions on others in comparison to how much time they spend accepting their faults and trying to improve on them. Let your answer to this help guide you to whether or not this person is deserving of your time, love and attention.

Red Flag #5 - They 'Jokingly' Insult and Offend You

'Jokey' insults or slurs are brushed off as 'banter' or 'having fun'. If your partner insults you, and your reaction is to be offended, they'll make you feel like you're dull or can't take a joke. This should make you question: *does my partner not care how they make me feel? Are they trying to degrade, upset or humiliate me?*

As with all of these red flags, your instinct plays a big part in answering this. There is a difference between being insensitive and purposefully making someone feel hurt. The way you can work out if your partner has simply overstepped the 'joke' mark into 'mean' territory or if they are knowingly trying to upset you is by confronting them about it. Their answer or reaction should tell you what you need to know.

If they are shocked that they've upset you and are mortified that their misplaced joke has offended you, then they'll show it - they'll try to make amends and show you that their intention wasn't to hurt you. They won't brush you off as being sensitive or unable to take a joke. They won't laugh at you or be condescending about your feelings and emotions. They won't make you feel as if you're being irrational, hypersensitive or overly critical.

If one of your partner's 'jokes' has upset you and they react in such a disrespectful and patronizing way, then they've answered your question. They either don't care how they make you feel or possibly worse - they care enough to want to make you feel degraded or offended. The latter is the warning sign of a very callous, manipulative and dangerous abuser.

It's also worth thinking about the context and subject of the 'jokes' that have hurt you. What were they about? Did they belittle your accomplishments or achievements? Were they about something your partner knows you're insecure about? Did they allude to something you've told them in discretion?

An emotionally healthy, caring, loving partner ought to know when they're overstepping the mark with the topics they use to have banter with you. However, sometimes people are a little insensitive and don't always think before their mouth runs away from them. To help you decide if their offensive jokes should serve as a red flag, consider the number of times they offend you 'jokingly', the topic of the jibes as well as your partner's reaction to your upset once you confront them about it. This should help you better gauge their intentions from their lackluster joking.

If it turns out your other half has just been less-than-tactful but didn't mean to offend, then they ought to take your upset on board and understand where you draw the line where their joke telling is concerned.

Red Flag #6 - They Use Social Media as a Tool to Make You Jealous

We can't escape the modern way of communicating, where we commune through our screens to convey how we feel or think. It's hard to remember a world where communication was primal and face-to-face. Now, in the era of social media, we have to read between the lines of ambiguous status', understand the intent behind the quotes or memes that people post and keep up with 'relationship status' changes. This, of course, can make dating and relationships that bit more difficult; understanding your other half and knowing their true feelings and intentions can be skewed by social media.

A narcissist or manipulator will utilize social media to make you feel like your relationship isn't as stable or secure as you were lead to believe. They won't do this immediately, however - firstly they make you feel like all of their thoughts and attention are on you; that you're on a pedestal and no one can or will compare. They make you feel safe, cared for and adored initially.

Then, as the relationship goes on, they'll use their social media profiles as a tool to pull that rug from under you. From once feeling safe and stable, this unsteady feeling of *are they still interested in me?'* is just what an abuser needs to make their spouse chase after them and run after the attention they once gave so freely. This will fuel the ego of the abuser.

Ambiguous status', questionable videos or pictures and inside jokes (that you're not in on) posted by your partner may be used to make you feel jealous. Querying these dubious posts with your partner will likely be met with an answer suggesting you're crazy or protesting that you're taking things the wrong way or being a psycho. Of course, this cover of innocence is just another layer they add to fuel your unsteadiness about yourself and to make you question your perceptions.

You may find that your partner uses other people on their social media profiles as bait. For example, mine used an ex-partner of his. He and his ex weren't on speaking terms when we met, and he told me she was awful towards him, treated him like dirt and was the reason he was so insecure. They were, however, still friends on social media because 'he was friends with her brother and didn't want to make it awkward between them', so I didn't probe further on this. After a while, this denounced ex soon began posting on his wall, joking about things I didn't understand because I 'wasn't there', or posting a picture of a memory she'd seen.

Predictably, I was anxious that she was creeping back on the scene and wanted reassurance that my ex wanted me, not his ex-partner. When I tried to broach this, he told me I was being silly, jealous or that I was acting crazy. However, I noticed that he tended to each of her status' or posts to his wall immediately, replying within minutes. When I would post to his page or post a picture, it would go ignored, or he would see to other people's activity before he acknowledged mine. This was conflicting with what he would say to me; that I was special, the most important person to him and his best friend. So, of course, I felt confused, upset, jealous and craving his attention and adoration. As you probably know, this made me chase him all the more, giving him the validation and ego boost he was after, all whilst making me feel as if I had to fight for a place in his heart.

Be wary of any social media posts that may provoke a sense of jealousy or rivalry in you - they may be the bait to make you feel just that.

Red Flag #7 - Feeling on Edge Around Them

You feel on edge when you're around your newfound partner; maybe you can't quite put your finger on why, but you feel like you're nervous about your partner's reactions to or interpretations of the things you say or do.

You want them to still like you and maintain their keen interest in you, but you're aware that there's something conditional about the way they feel about you-you know that if you inadvertently upset them, that may spell trouble for the relationship and their feelings for you moving forward.

Feeling like you're on eggshells or anxious around your partner often means that you feel like their affection and adoration of you is dangled above you like a carrot; you almost feel like you're competing for their love and attention. If you play by their rules and keep them happy, you get the carrot. If you dare to inadvertently upset them, the carrot is flung away, out of your sight completely. Unless, of course, they choose to bring it back into your view.

The antsy, highly-strung feelings you experience with a new partner shouldn't be negative ones like this; they should fuel your excitement and passion for the relationship. You shouldn't be feeling like you're on an emotional tightrope.

Feeling on edge is an early red flag you should listen to. If your partner doesn't make you feel like you can say certain things or behave in a particular way, because it'll upset them, then listen to the fretful feelings you sometimes have when you're around your other half. They're serving you a warning: this person doesn't calm or soothe you - quite the opposite.

Red Flag #8 - They're Surrounded by Potential Partners or Former Partners

Being friends with an ex isn't a crime, nor is it uncommon, especially if there are children involved. However, there is a difference between being amicable with an ex and remaining friendly with them, and appearing to surround yourself with them and other potential partners.

This can be made all the more hurtful if your partner brags about how they know such-and-such would love to sleep with them, that they know so-and-so has wanted to be with them for ages and how they can have anyone if they wanted.

What can be worse is if they remain in contact with an ex, and tell you that said ex would 'love to have them back'. Of course, your partner might assure you that there's nothing to worry about, but they'll know they've already planted that toxic seed in your head. That wasn't an accident - they intentionally leave you feeling insecure, cast-aside and helpless with their contradicting words and actions. Your partner giving off the impression that they're sought after and in high demand only serves to make you feel undeserving of them, and as such, feel lucky that they're with you at all.

I've been through this kind of emotional torture, and I can attest to the fact that it leaves you harboring lots of ugly feelings: rage, jealousy, anger, frustration, insecurity, and instability to name a few. My ex would let me know about all of the other women he was 'friends' with who were attracted to him, who flirted with him, who he was a 'shoulder to cry on' for, whom he once had a fling with, and it would eat me up inside that I was only one of many who held a place in his heart.

Anyone worth your time wouldn't intentionally make you feel this way. They wouldn't want to make you feel less than others or like you had to fight for their attention.

If your partner is keen to let you know just how in-demand they are by surrounding themselves with people who are (or were) conquests or lovers and enjoy making you feel upset and jealous over that, then not only should that big, red flag be waving, but so should you - waving goodbye to that kind of toxicity in your life.

Red Flag #9 - Only You Can See Their Dark Side

It's incredibly frustrating when you can see right through someone and no-one else can see what you can. When someone has a dark, sneaky or mean side that you've been exposed to but nobody else has, it's maddening when no-one else can possibly imagine that person being anything except the 'nice' person they portray themselves as. There's no exception when that person you can see right through is the person you're dating.

Be wary of someone who only shows off their darker side to you. It could be their true colors. Others may think that your other half is a nice, funny, kind and unassuming individual, whereas you've seen that to not always be the case.

My ex would get mad at me for 'saying the wrong thing' in front of people, but he wouldn't mention anything whilst we were in the company of others. He'd wait until we got home and unleash his torrent of nastiness upon me - making me feel stupid, berating me for saying the wrong thing and being cold and distant. He'd punish me for something I'd unwittingly done, but he'd still play the 'nice guy' in front of company.

He would wait until we got home to rage at me for laughing at someone else's joke for too long, and accuse me of 'flirting' with them. He would scold me for being late out of work when he came to pick me up, but he wouldn't show his anger in front of my colleagues - he would wait until I was in the car, and he'd relentlessly go on about how my lack of timekeeping showed him disrespect.

Other people couldn't even begin to imagine what my ex was like in private, because he did such a good job of not allowing his mask to slip in public. He came across as helpful, pleasant and understanding to the outside world, but as the relationship developed, the mask he wore in front of me began to slip, and I was exposed to more and more of his mean, cold and nasty side. However, he still maintained his good guy persona to almost everyone else.

Red Flag #10 - Inability to Put Themselves in Your Shoes

If your partner makes you feel upset, confused or uncertain, it's healthy to be able to talk about this with them; to explain where your feelings stem from and why you feel that way. The result of this usually sees your partner aim to justify themselves and explain why they believe you shouldn't feel that way or have your partner look at things from your point of view and understand where they went wrong. Either way, by broaching how you feel with them, you and your partner ought to be able to have a healthy, constructive conversation about how you feel and strive to see each other's point of view.

However, if you find that your other half can't put themselves in your shoes, or anyone else's, then this is something to take heed of. It's not just an annoying character flaw or stubborn personality trait, it's a sign of something much more sinister.

It can spell trouble ahead for your relationship, as not only will you be hitting a brick wall when you try to explain how they make you feel, you'll waste plenty of your time desperately trying to get them to see things from your point of view.

The inability to put themselves in another person's shoes can be an indication of that person having a narcissistic personality disorder. A person with NPD tends to be unable to relate to the feelings and emotions of others, and their primary concern is their own wants and needs. To a narcissist, their significant other is a mere extension of themselves, and being in a relationship with one will not only drain you, but it'll also strip you of your sense of self. Be careful of this warning sign before you find your emotional health is sucked out of you.

Red Flag #11 - They Accuse You of Emotions That They Are Directly Causing

A big, big red flag to make sure you don't ignore is this one: if your significant other is berating you for emotions you're feeling because their intentional provoking of them.

This is an early warning sign of a manipulator, and it can be hard to spot straight away because they'll deny all knowledge of how they're making you upset or insecure. They'll blast you for being clingy, too needy or a psycho when you confront them about how they're making you feel, even though it's their actions that are making you feel that way.

When I sought out recovery from my abusive ex, one of the first things I did was seek out people who'd been through similar traumatic experiences. Little did I expect that when I did so, we'd all have extremely similar recounts of how our exes treated us and make us feel. One of the common denominators we'd all share is this red flag. We'd all have almost identical stories of how our ex had blatantly flirted with someone else in front of us, yet palmed us off as a psycho when we confronted them about it. For many of us, our exes would disappear for days, ignoring our attempts at contact, only to call us 'needy' when they do eventually get back in touch.

If this sounds similar to your situation, it's time to reassess the individual who is making you feel this way. Someone who'll knowingly and deliberately make you feel insecure and low is not only not worth a jot of your time, but they're also exhibiting signs of being a manipulative abuser. Don't just take this red flag as a 'proceed with caution', take it as a stark warning that this individual is toxic.

Red Flag #12 - They Focus on Your Mistakes (But Ignore Their Own)

Do you find that if your partner lets you down, turns up late or falls through on a promise that they'll retaliate by bringing your own flaws or mistakes to your attention? Instead of being apologetic or understanding your upset, they remind you of the times you've made a mistake. They won't accept that they're in the wrong, but they'll happily roll out all of the times you were in the wrong - listing them off one by one should you dare mention a mistake they've made.

The very first time I went on an 'official' date with my ex I was just under fifteen minutes late as the taxi I'd ordered to take me there was slightly late, then we hit some unexpected traffic on the way. At the time, I messaged him to let him know I was on my way and how sorry I was that I was running a little late. He replied it was fine, and didn't seem bothered by this at the time. However, as the relationship developed, I came to realize he was bad at timekeeping and turning up when he was expected. If I dared bring this up to him or question him about it, he'd bring up the time I was late to our very first date. This, he told me, set the scene for the entire relationship, and showed him just how much I cared about him: If I *couldn't even be on time for our most important date - why should I stick my neck out to be on time for anything if you can't do the same'*, was his usual reply.

Even years into our relationship, this was still the event he would use to turn the tables on me if I confronted him about being late or not showing up.

If you're with someone who tries to brush their mistakes off as being yours or somebody else's fault all the time, be attentive to that flag. If they're quick to turn the conversation back to you if you're trying to bring up something they've done to upset you, think to yourself why they may be doing that; do they know they're in the wrong but would rather make you feel bad than own up to their mistakes?

Red Flag #13 - They're Hypercritical

Beware of anyone, especially your other half, if they're the ultimate hypocrite.

It may start off seemingly small and nitpicky; they may bring up how you overdone the vegetables for dinner or how you never seem to make their coffee just how they like it. They may even mention these things in an apparently jokey manner, trying to appear like they're jesting with you instead of subtly criticizing you. This covert criticism soon reveals itself to be more sinister than you were first led to believe. Little nitpicks soon manifest into full-blown accusatory criticisms and slurs, which represent the high standards and levels of perfection your other half expects of you.

As I mentioned, it doesn't start off this way: it begins with smaller, more superficial critiques that are often masked as jokes or banter. If you notice this has become a habit for your other half, then allow it to offer you some foresight on what may be in store for the future of your relationship.

This red flag spells the warning signs of a partner who, as the relationship goes on, will use your apparent shortfalls or mistakes as a way to remind you of their expectations of you. If you don't upkeep their scrupulous standards then be prepared for an onslaught of criticism.

The frustrating thing about this red flag is that, whilst your other half is being hypocritical of you, there's a good chance that they're not honoring their own high standards. For all you're expected to be 'perfect' - show respect, be monogamous, truthful and adoring - your other half is likely doing as they please in those aspects.

Red Flag #14 - They Have Different Personas for Different People

It can sometimes almost feel as if your partner forgets who they're supposed to be around when they're around you. You've noticed that they interchange their persona depending on who they're around at that time - they can transform their entire personality to blend in with the audience they have at any given time.

This is something you've likely noticed by accident. Your other half wouldn't want to be exposed as a fraud or manipulator, so if they have different personas for different people, they usually try to keep this under wraps. However, even for the most veteran manipulator, their mask does occasionally slip, and they'll accidentally use the wrong persona in front of you. If you've been exposed to this mask slip, or believe that something about their personality around others doesn't quite add up, then don't let this observation fall by the wayside; acknowledge it as potential warning behavior that may be a red flag to expose your partner's true colors.

It can come as a bit of a shock when you see another side to your partner's personality. It's unsettling when your spouse acts like a completely different person in front of other people, almost like you don't know their true personality at all. Be on alert if this is the case for you.

Red Flag #15 - You're in Fear of Them Leaving You at Any Time

A healthy relationship sees issues resolved by communication, even if that sometimes means they argue. Although arguing isn't idealistic, it's normal and human to argue when your emotions get the best of you - even the healthiest of couples will tell you they argue from time to time.

However, if you're on eggshells when you argue with your other half, then you should question why that is. If one of your answers is that you're afraid *'this argument could be the last'* because of how they dangle the relationship over you during heated disagreements, then you need to consider the future of the partnership.

If you feel like broaching topics that need discussing with your partner may cause them to end the relationship, use the fear that gives you to help you understand *why* that's the case: is it because they don't care enough to address their own behavior, and they'd rather end or jeopardize the relationship they have with you instead of having a difficult conversation?

If your other half has made it clear that certain subjects, conversations or 'deep talks' are a sure-fire way to get them running for the hills, this is a huge predictor of an unstable and potentially narcissistic relationship.

In my case, my ex would dangle our relationship over my head if I dared try and confront him about his behavior towards me. If I tried to talk to him to resolve issues, understand why he did certain things or let him know how he made me feel, I knew this was a risky territory. He could, and often would, use this as a way to walk out of the relationship or get me begging for him to stay with me. I'd often be the one giving him my apologies and forgiveness, just so he didn't end the relationship.

Now I can see it from a stronger, more emotionally secure place, I can see that this behavior from him was a way to exert his control over me. He knew I'd not be able to express myself freely or be open about my feelings as I cared about him (and our relationship) too much to jeopardize the possibility of him ending it for good.

Red Flag #16 - They Want You to Read Their Mind

If you've done something wrong or upset your spouse, it's reasonable to expect them to let you know what you've done (in a healthy, constructive way, of course).

However, if you find that your other half is expecting you to read their mind and you should instinctively know what you've done, then view this as a huge, manically-waving red flag.

For example, if you get the silent treatment for a few days, they ignore you or are noticeably cold towards you, this may be your partner 'punishing' you for something you've done to upset them. They might be making you pay for not remembering the plans they had that they told you nothing about, or they might be penalizing you for accidentally telling their mother a story about them being drunk - when they make their mother believe they don't touch alcohol. Whatever you've done to upset them, being made pay by the punishment of silence is a red flag in itself. Couple it with the fact that your spouse expects you to know, without them telling you, what you've done, is a *huge* red flag.

If you've noticed your partner doing this, then you may have also noticed that there's always a 'victim' story to accompany their silent treatment and expectation of you being able to read their mind. Whatever you've done to hurt them is something you should have known not to do, because it's something that triggers their upset or sadness.

Red Flag #17 - A Need for Attention

We all need attention and it's certainly something we should expect to receive from our significant other. However, an emotionally healthy individual only expects this within reason, and they don't utilize their partner's attention to boot their own ego.

If your other half is constantly clamoring for attention, sucking your energy until it's drained and wanting to consume your whole life, then you may be in a relationship with an emotional vampire. This selfish 'all about me' trait is something you need to avoid if you want a healthy relationship that'll allow both of you to flourish.

Their constant demand for your attention and affection appears to be impossible to satisfy, but it may fill you with some comfort if you feel like you're the only person they seek that attention from. However, whilst it appears this way at first, you may soon realize that they seek out attentiveness from other people - other people can also give them the same as you can, and have the same results as you do. Of course, this is bound to make you feel inadequate or like 'just another person' to your partner. To a narcissistic manipulator, that's exactly what you are - just another person to get their supply from.

Red Flag #18 - They Make You Feel Like a Chore

Once upon a time, you were the apple of your partner's eye. They adored you, and they weren't afraid to show it. You were lavished with a great big bomb of love, and you didn't expect that that'd ever change. You didn't foresee your bubble of love to be burst, least of all by the same person who's got you wrapped up in their daydream of love.

However, if you're now taken aback by your partner's sudden boredom of you, their unexpected disinterest, or their newfound hostility and coldness towards you, this could be a warning of trouble ahead. Whilst we can all be a little distant from time to time, especially if we're stressed or have worries, you'll be able to use your gut instinct to gauge what kind of cold shoulder your partner is giving you.

If they make you feel like being with you is a chore or they become annoyed by your presence, then you need to reassess your position in your courtship. The sudden disinterest of continuing the romantic relationship you once shared is a common trait that narcissistic abusers utilize to 'devalue' you. They bombard you with love and attention, then strip it away at their own discretion, choosing not to give you an explanation of why.

This red flag is the middle segment of the cycle of narcissism. A narcissist will idealize, devalue and then discard their victim. Making you feel like a burden, a nuisance or a weight on their shoulders is an abusers way to make you feel devalued.

The devaluation phase is a confusing, frustrating and heartbreaking time to endure. Your partner is on and off with their interest in you and the relationship they once pursued and doted on. Your insecurities are flaring up, yet you will still cling to the memory and hope of the 'pedestal phase' you had at the very beginning of the relationship. It's quite probable that you'll be in denial and think that the 'old' love interest you once knew will return - the interested, love-struck and passionate one that you thought you'd met. You may even blame yourself, which is what an abuser would want – you tell yourself that you just need to give your partner a little bit of time and some more space, support their independence more and be less clingy... but those thoughts are simply a defense mechanism. Your thought of denial are wrong - it's not you to blame, and the perfec partner you once had is unlikely to return.

Red Flag #19 - They Talk About Their Ex Partners (Quite a Lot)

Be wary of how your partner describes their ex(es). Whilst we all have bad exes, and a lot of the time we probably don't have shining things to say about our exes, we don't feel the need to let everyone know about how horrible they were - most of all our new partner. If you find that your partner engages you in lots of negative conversations about their ex, then heed this ginormous red flag wafting in front of you. Can you imagine what your partner would say about you if they met someone new; how they'd describe you, your flaws and how they may twist events that'd occurred.

If your other half if constantly looking for cues to berate or talk about their ex, then it's not looking good for your future. If you know lots of information about your partner's ex, arguments they've had, places they've been or things that you don't really need to know, then it could be time to consider why that is. If your partner is talking about their ex a lot of the time, it could be that they're not quite over the relationship or they're bitter about it ending. On the more sinister side, your partner may be projecting; all of the vile and horrible things they tell you their ex did may be the precise things your partner did during his ex-relationship. The lying cheat he portrays his ex as may just be the person he was during that relationship.

Be wary of someone who sees no issue in oversharing information about their ex and the relationship they once shared.

Red Flag #20 - They Never or Rarely Say 'Sorry'

We're human. We make mistakes. We mess up. We don't always get it right. We sometimes say or do the wrong thing. It happens, and there's no getting away from that fact - but we can take ownership of our errors and say sorry when there is an apology in order. This is a primal urge we have to right our wrongs and try to make things okay again if we mess up.

However, tread very carefully if you've noticed that your other half seems incapable of saying sorry or owning their mistakes. Not only does it say a lot about their character, but it's also a warning for the way in which your relationship is heading: if there so unapologetic in the early stages of your relationship, can you bare to imagine how they'll treat you a decade down the line?

Of course, apologies do vary in their significance but do pay attention to when or if your partner chooses to give one. If they bump into someone else in a bar, do they reply with a 'sorry' or do they berate the other person for not watching where they're going?

The above example is relatively small fry when it comes to how hurtful and emotionally distressing a 'non-apologiser' can be.

****

I hope these twenty red flags have in someway helped you navigate your way towards a healthier relationship, decide that you deserve better treatment or have stopped you from entering into a toxic partnership. I hope it's given you some knowledge and cautionary advice to keep in mind whilst traversing through the often-confusing world of dating.

As a former victim of abuse, I understand if you feel like I'm being hypervigilant when it comes to dating. You may feel that I see everyone and every action as a threat or trigger warning. After all, if you've been abused by those closest to you for a big chunk of your life, how can you really trust anyone? But, I do, and I never stopped giving my trust; only now, I've developed a fine-tuned intuition and I follow my gut instinct. It's not about whether or not you should trust. I fully believe you *should* trust until proven you shouldn't.

These red flags are only useful to you if you follow your intuition and primal gut inclination. Your instinct has allowed you to pick up on these red flags, it's now up to you how you follow up on that. My greatest downfall and the downfall of so many others I know who've been abused is to not listen to what the hunches and gut instincts were saying. For too long, I passed them off as my own paranoia, being too unnecessarily distrusting or believing my ex when he told me I was 'crazy'. The lack of respect I had for my own intuition created a vulnerability in me that allowed me to fall into the cycle of abuse.

Most of all, I'd like you to have taken away a brand new faith in your own gut instinct. You're not crazy, you're not 'making things up out of nowhere', and you're not paranoid. You're listening to what the feeling in your bones is telling you, and I can assure you of this; whilst it may not always be 100% accurate, it's never far off. Have faith in your own intuitiveness because it's got your best interests at heart.

To end this book, I'd like to offer the twenty-six relationship 'green flags' myself and a group of seven other good friends of mine came up with one night when we were discussing the content of this book. To lighten the mood and share our combined knowledge, we all input what our own 'green flags' are for a potential partner - what signs we have to tell us to 'go!' rather than 'stop right there!' when considering the future of the relationship.

Whilst this list isn't exhaustive (and, do let me know if you have any suggestions of your own), these green flags serve to be the solid basis on which a healthy, happy and emotionally stable relationship needs to flourish on.

26 Relationship Green Flags

1. You know your partner's best friend and you're able to identify lots of good qualities about them.

2. You find it easy and natural to be playful with your partner.

3. You trust your partner's ideas and trust them to come from a good place.

4. In some ways, you'd like to obtain some of your partner's qualities, i.e., their patience or their listening skill.s

5. When you disagree or have a debate, your partner can still acknowledge your logical and reasonable input into the conversation. Likewise, you can also admit when they are right.

6. You admit to each other that you think about one another when you're apart.

7. You have a primal, gut instinct that you can trust your partner in every way.

8. Your partner is happy and enthusiastic when you succeed at something or have good news - they want to share your good times as well as be there for the bad.

9. Your partner has confided their biggest goals, dreams, and aspirations in life; this shows they trust you enough to put themselves out there with the possibility of failure. They know that, even if they don't get the outcome they want, you'll still be here.

10. You can talk to each other about the things you've overcome as a couple, and it won't cause arguments. For example, jealousy or miscommunication.

11. You're affectionate with each other every day.

12. You feel trusting and comfortable enough to let your partner know your biggest fears and worries.

13. You and your partner can share embarrassing stories with each other.

14. You never (or rarely), express abhorrence for your partner by rolling your eyes, swearing at them, or calling them psychotic or crazy.

15. Your partner enjoys you exploring your hobbies or goals, even if this means they have to stay at home or have limited involvement.

16. Even when you argue with your other half, you still have full confidence that your spouse cares about your thoughts, feelings, and opinions.

17. Your partner readily makes their thoughts and feelings open to you.

18. Your partner frequently expresses their admiration for you and the person you are.

19. You feel like you and your partner are like teammates.

20. You've felt trusting enough to tell your other half about trauma from your past, and their reaction was kind and supportive. They'd never use that trauma as a way to manipulate or control you.

21. Your partner is happy to talk to you about things you're passionate about, even if they have little to know knowledge or interest in the subject; they'll be happy to discuss your passion with you because it makes you happy.

22. Your partner respects your relationships with your family and friends and views them as important; they encourage you to maintain healthy relationships.

23. You and your other half have fun. It's easy, natural and organic part of your relationship.

24. Your partner is receptive to your ideas; they'll try their suggestions.

25. You feel butterflies when you think about returning home to them - you're not afraid of what might greet you when you get home.

26. When you feel worried, upset or stressed, you know you can turn toward your partner for comfort and understanding. You know you don't have to deal with it alone.

Don't miss out!

Visit the website below and you can sign up to receive emails whenever Lauren Kozlowski publishes a new book. There's no charge and no obligation.

https://books2read.com/r/B-A-PTHI-OOFZ

BOOKS 2 READ

Connecting independent readers to independent writers.

About the Publisher

Escape The Narcissist is about helping you find your self-worth, offering you some thought provoking ideas to change your life and aiding you in revitalizing your relationships.

With that in mind, Escape The Narcissist has one core relationship we want to focus on: the one you have with yourself.

Our website was born from a place of darkness. We've all, at some point in our lives, been on the receiving end of ill treatment from others. From being a victim of a narcissistic relationship to being mistreated by those who should protect us and not being shown the respect we deserve, these toxic relationships can affect us more than we realise.

Whilst the people behind the content of our site and books all have their own ideas and stories, they have one thing in common: they've all overcome toxicity in their lives and want to share their story.

The content of the stories, pieces of advice and actionable life changes within this site all aim to inspire, provoke a healthier way of thinking, and help to heal any negative effects you've been left with at the hands of other people.

escapethenarcissist.com

CPSIA information can be obtained
at www.ICGtesting.com
Printed in the USA
BVHW040202281021
620169BV00005B/138

9 781393 271536